美好嘅 童年
CHILDHOOD
Is a GREAT JOURNEY

by
ANDREA VOON

I0528796

好媽咪，請坐低，陪我哋玩煮飯仔。

食乜嘢？慢慢揀，套餐今日大優惠。

凍檸茶，熱咖啡，煎牛扒，烤火雞……

食甜品，送雪糕，蛋糕好食又好睇。

Hot soup? Cooked. Turkey? Cooked.
Let's preheat the big oven,
and bake a birthday cake.

Tea and coffee... Cupcakes and ice creams...
We're ready for a tea party
when mummy takes her break.

洗切煮炒好手勢，甜酸苦辣啱口味。

sai² cit³ zyu² caau² hou² sau² sai³　　tim⁴ syun¹ fu² laat⁶ ngaam¹ hau² mei⁶

愛心餸菜最開胃，食得健康唔怕肥。

oi³ sam¹ sung³ coi³ zeoi³ hoi¹ wai⁶　　sik⁶ dak¹ gin⁶ hong¹ m⁴ paa³ fei⁴

Washing and cooking while sipping on our milkshake.

Eating and laughing until we have a stomach ache.

zo² sau² hing¹　jau⁶ sau² cung⁵　hak¹ gin⁶　baak⁶ gin⁶ ding¹ ding¹ hoeng²

左手輕，右手重，黑鍵、白鍵叮叮響。

zo² bin¹ aat³　jau⁶ bin¹ sou³　gou¹ jam¹　dai¹ jam¹ hing¹ hing¹ joeng⁴

左邊壓，右邊掃，高音、低音輕輕揚。

taan⁴ gong³ kam⁴　taan⁴ git³ taa¹　zaa¹ zyu⁶ zi¹ mai¹ gou¹ seng¹ coeng³

彈鋼琴，彈吉他，揸住支咪高聲唱。

paak³ paak³ sau²　daap⁶ daap⁶ goek³　coeng³ jyun⁴ jat¹ coeng⁴ jau⁶ jat¹ coeng⁴

拍拍手，踏踏腳，唱完一場又一場。

5

White keys, black keys... Do-re-mi-fa-so-
Let's form a music band, and play our favorite song.
High notes, low notes... So-fa-mi-re-do-
Tapping and clapping, and repeat all day long.

haau¹ tung⁴ bat⁶　　daa² lo⁴ gu²　　baa¹ leoi⁵ mou⁵ kwan⁴ tam⁴ tam² zyun³

敲銅鈸， 打鑼鼓， 芭蕾舞裙氹氹轉。

sau² laai¹ sau²　　zyun³ hyun¹ hyun¹　　coeng³ coeng³ tiu³ tiu³ hei³ m⁴ cyun²

手拉手， 轉圈圈， 唱唱跳跳氣唔喘。

One, two, three, four...
Sing our happy song loud and strong.

Move it... Groove it...
Skip around a circle, and dance along.

Tweezers? **Set!** Bandages? **Set!**

Daddy sprained his ankle in a soccer game.

Stethoscope? **Cleaned**! Thermometer? **Cleaned**!

We're ready for the next patient, **PLEASE** call out her name.

急診室，多病人，請你耐心等一陣。

量血壓，探下熱，醫生輪住嚟睇診。

爹地唔小心扭親，隻腳嚴重傷到筋。

打支針，再包紮，后日記得嚟覆診。

can¹ can¹ mui⁴ mui² zok³ gam² mou⁶　　jau⁶ o¹　jau⁶ au² tau⁴ wan⁴ wan⁴
親親妹妹作感冒，　又屙又嘔頭暈暈。

sik⁶ jyun⁴ joek⁶　　jam² daam⁶ seoi²　　fan³ seng² zau⁶ wui⁵ hou² zing¹ san⁴
食完藥，　飲啖水，　瞓醒就會好精神。

Here are your medicines,
PLEASE drink more water.

Take a good bed rest,
and you'll be better.

12

媽咪揸住購物單，帶埋我哋去行街。

推車仔，來掃貨，睇下有乜嘢好買。

Oranges? **Yes!** Apples? **No!**
Let's be a smart helper
at the mini-mart.

揀水果，揀零食，我同妹妹來鬥快。

睇質地，睇價錢，邊個牌子可信賴？

Cookies? **Here**! Fresh milk? **There**!

We're ready for the checkout with a heavy cart.

新玩具，好牌子，平靚正，先抵買。

san¹ wun⁶ geoi⁶　hou² paai⁴ zi²　peng⁴ leng³ zeng³　sin¹ dai² maai⁵

一百蚊，唔使找，大買特買真痛快。

jat¹ baak³ man¹　m⁴ sai² zaau²　daai⁶ maai⁵ dak⁶ maai⁵ zan¹ tung³ faai³

Which toy is cheaper?
Which treat is tastier?

One hundred dollars,
and **THANK YOU** dear cashier.

lok6 daai6 jyu5 gwaat3 daai6 fung1 daai6 gaa1 ci1 maai4 waan2 jau4 hei3

落大雨，颳大風，大家黐埋玩游戲。

jat1 gaa1 jan4 jiu3 wo4 hei3 m4 zaang1 syu1 jeng4 m4 dau3 hei3

一家人，要和氣，唔爭輸贏唔鬥氣。

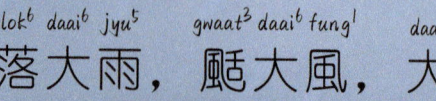

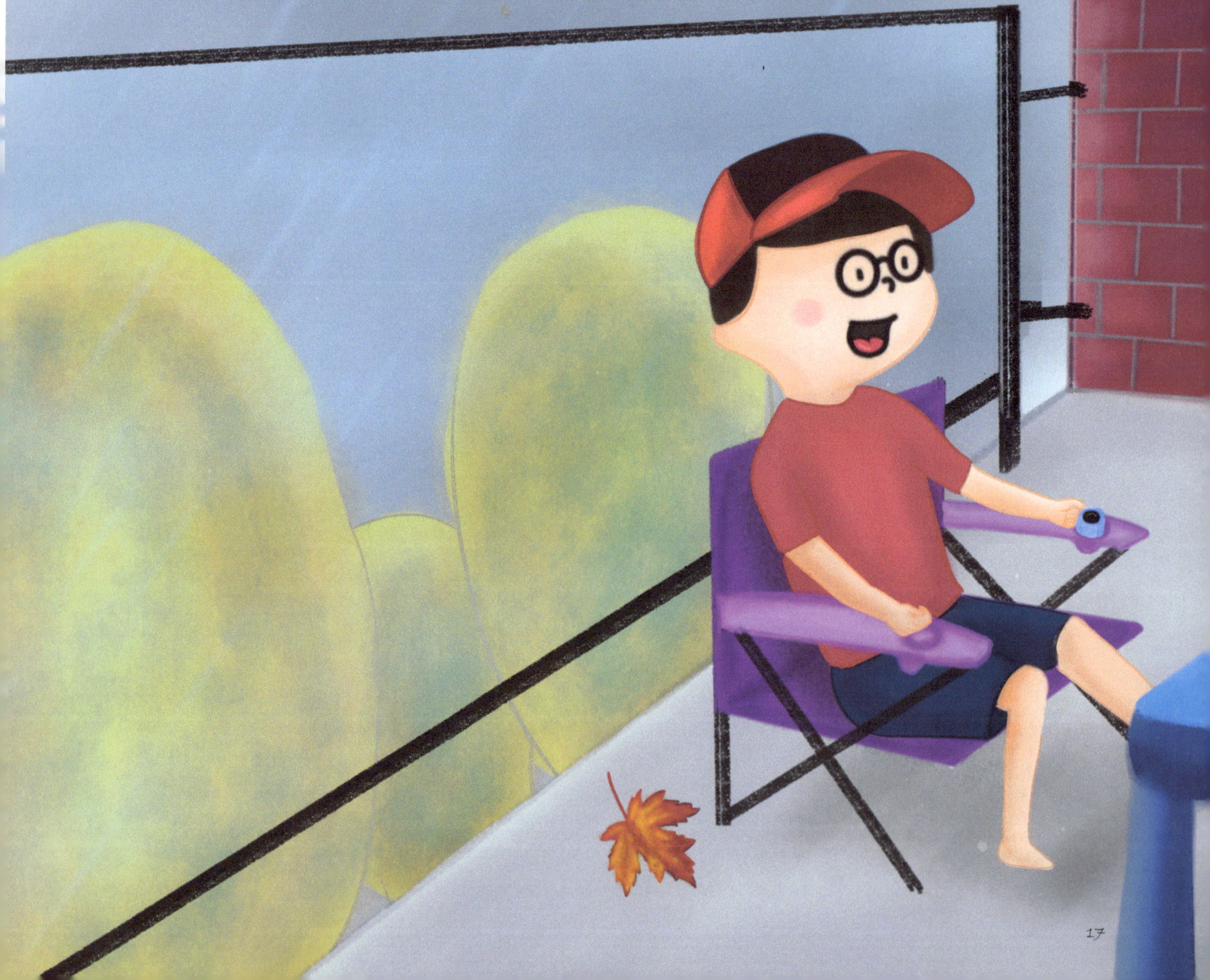

Red or yellow; Green or blue?
Let's choose a fun game to kick-start our date.

Whose turn is it now? Who is the winner?

The sky is gloomy, yet we're doing **GREAT**!

瞓覺前，要刷牙，爛牙唔會纏住你。
（fan³ gaau³ cin⁴，jiu³ caat³ ngaa⁴，laan⁶ ngaa⁴ m⁴ wui⁵ cin⁴ zyu⁶ nei⁵）

冚好被，錫翻啖，噩夢唔會黐住你。
（kam² hou² pei⁵，sek³ faan¹ daam⁶，ok³ mung⁶ m⁴ wui⁵ ci¹ zyu⁶ nei⁵）

Up and down, in and out...
Brush your little teeth twice a day.

CAVITIES! Keep at bay!
Call it a day, and hit the hay.

19

企直直，咪亂嘟，身高體重要記低。
kei⁵ zik⁶ zik⁶　mai¹ lyun⁶ juk¹　san¹ gou¹ tai² cung⁵ jiu³ gei³ dai¹

量一量，磅一磅，睇吓你哋乖唔乖。
loeng² jat¹ loeng⁴　bong⁶ jat¹ bong⁶　tai² haa⁵ nei⁵ dei⁶ gwaai¹ m⁴ gwaai¹

唔揀食，唔曳曳，爹地媽咪就錫晒。
m⁴ gaan² sik⁶　m⁴ jai¹ jai¹　de¹ dei⁶ maa¹ mi⁴ zau⁶ sek³ saai³

眨吓眼，就長大，時間過得真係快。
zaam² haa⁵ ngaan⁵　zau⁶ zoeng² daai⁶　si⁴ gaan³ gwo³ dak¹ zan¹ hai⁶ faai³

Veggies and fruits; Eggs and meats.
I'm **NOT** picky, and I clean up my plate!

Did I grow **taller**? Did I get **heavier**?
As tall as Mum and Dad! I just **CAN'T** wait!

me¹ syu¹ baau¹　　heoi³ faan¹ hok⁶　　min⁶ daai³ siu³ jung⁴ gong² baai¹ baai³

孭書包，去返學，面帶笑容講拜拜。

ziu¹ ziu¹ sau²　　laam⁵ jat¹ laam⁵　　hoi¹ hoi¹ sam¹ sam¹ m⁴ nau² gai²

招招手，攬一攬，開開心心唔扭計。

Lunch box? **Checked**!

Backpack? **Checked**!

"**HOORAY** for school!"

Teddy cheers.

Goodbye, Mom!
Goodbye, Dad!
Goodbye, little sis!
Shed **NO** tears!

美好嘅**童年**，

有屋企人喺身邊，

齊玩樂，齊歡笑。

25

CHILDHOOD is a great journey,

together with you,
we create lasting memories.

作者 Author

溫甘玉芬

當媽前，她是孩子們的甘老師，在常年暖和的熱帶雨林，與孩子一起學習中、英文，探索文字的奧秘；當媽後，她是孩子們的溫媽咪，在四季分明的北半球，與孩子一起感受春夏秋冬的更替，一起尋找美好的童年……

溫媽咪創作的靈感，源自於多年來的童言童語。

2021年，她成立了"溫室工作坊"，立志出版一系列的中、英雙語繪本，結合母語和第二語言，提倡親子趣讀。精通三語的溫媽咪理解每一種語言都有其獨特的藝術形式，因此創作的雙語繪本也各含韻味、各具特色。

Andrea Voon

Over the past few years, Andrea has learned and grown with her family as a full-time mother in Canada. Back in Malaysia, she worked as a teacher in Chinese immersion elementary school.
In 2021, Andrea started her journey as a self-publisher. Growing up in a multilingual environment, Andrea loves the beauty of languages on their own. She has the vision to publish picture books to support bilingual families in raising their children in English and Chinese reading.

To Derek, Eliana, Alayna & Magnus Dominus

with love -- Andrea V.

掃描聽粵語音頻
Scan for Cantonese Audio

Check out other bilingual picture books by Andrea Voon.

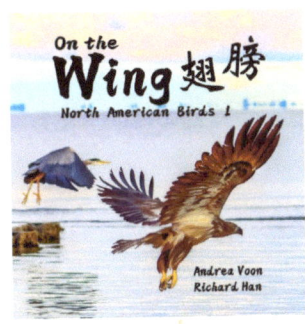

ISBN 978-1-998856-28-2
Text copyright © by 2025 Andrea Voon.
Illustration copyright ©2025 Andrea Voon, Yapp Shin Enn.

温室工作坊

www.ingramcontent.com/pod-product-compliance
Lightning Source LLC
Chambersburg PA
CBHW041501120626
46547CB00003B/506